A Day in the Life of a...

Baker

Carol Watson

W
FRANKLIN WATTS
NEW YORK • LONDON • SYDNEY

Richard is a baker.
At 3 a.m. he and his staff at the bakery start work making loaves, sausage rolls and pies for the day ahead.

First Richard mixes
the bread dough
in a huge bowl.

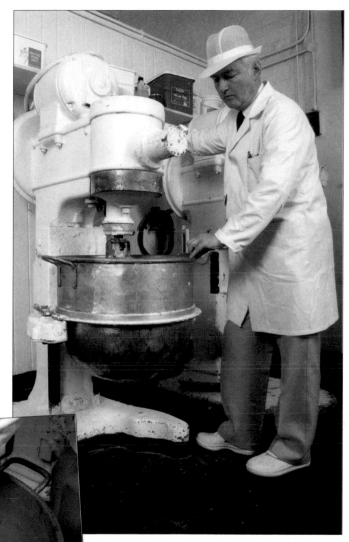

"This feels as if it's
the right texture,"
he says to himself.

3

When the dough is ready, Richard 'kneads' it until it is smooth and stretchy. He does this by pushing and pulling the dough before he shapes it into loaves.

4

Meanwhile Pete has made some pastry
for the tarts and pies.
He uses a giant rolling pin to roll
the pastry out flat.

While the
bread dough
is 'rising'
Richard helps
Pete to press
balls of pastry
into the
shape of
pastry cases.
These go
in the oven
to cook.

Once the dough has 'risen'
the loaves bake in the oven for 40 minutes.
When they are ready Richard uses a 'peel'
to take them out of the hot oven.

He leaves the trays
of bread to cool.

At 7 a.m. Richard goes into his office
to sort out the orders.
"How many large brown loaves
did you want?" he asks one of his customers.

8

Then Richard checks through
the orders with Ted, the delivery man.
"That's 24 large loaves — 12 white,
12 brown — and 20 sausage rolls," he says.
Ted loads up the van.

Next Richard and his staff
prepare the sandwiches and rolls.
"We sold out yesterday," Richard says.
"We need to make even more today."

In the shop Fred fills the shelves
ready for the morning's customers.
"That's the bread done," he says.
"Now I'll get the pies and sandwiches."

Richard's next job
is to put jam
into doughnuts
by injecting them
two by two.

Then he rolls the
doughnuts in sugar
ready to serve.

12

"Now it's time for the gingerbread men," says Richard.
He uses a metal shape to cut them out of the specially-made pastry.

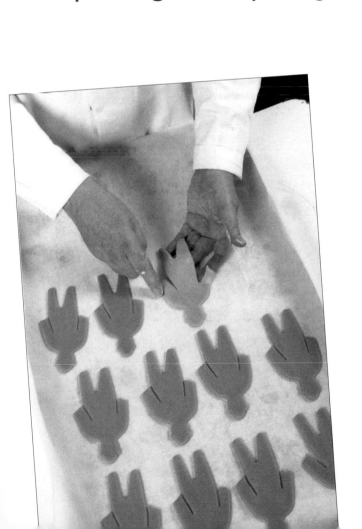

Then he lays them on a tray ready to bake in the oven.

13

Next Richard makes sugar mice
using blue sugar paste.
He gives each mouse a tail and
eyes made out of currants.

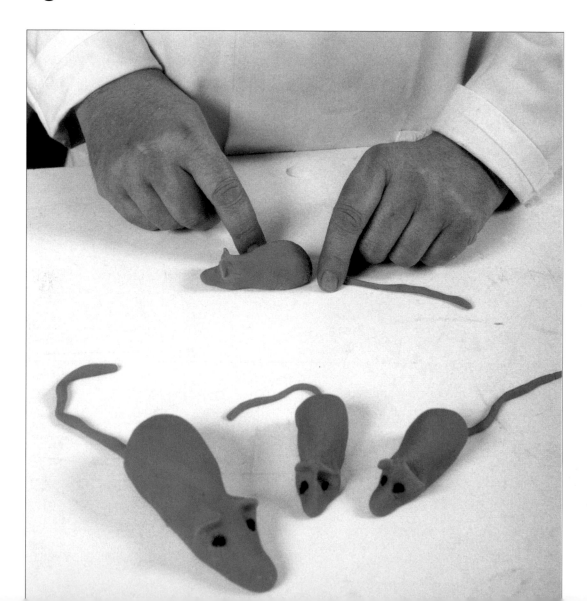

14

At 11 a.m. Richard decorates the cakes. He uses red sugar paste to make roses for some wedding cakes.

15

"I think pink flowers would look nice around the edge of this birthday cake," thinks Richard.

He uses an icing bag to 'pipe' on the flowers.

16

Rosemary packs the finished cakes into cake boxes. "These are ready for collection," she tells Richard.

When he has finished in the bakery
Richard helps in the shop.
"Can I have a gingerbread man, Mummy?"
asks one little girl.

"Here you are," says Richard.
"Now you can take him home."

By 5 p.m. it's time for
Richard to go home too.
He tidies his desk and
packs up for the day.

How to make a sugar mouse

You will need:

sugar paste (you can buy this at most supermarkets)

a mixing bowl

currants

edible food dye

rubber gloves

1. Put the sugar paste into the mixing bowl and mould it until it is smooth. Add a few drops of food dye and mix it into the paste until it is the colour you want.

2. Roll some of it into a ball and mould it into the shape of a mouse's body. Now make a smaller ball for the mouse's head.

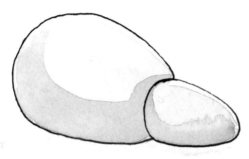

3. Join the head to the body and mould it so that it has a pointed nose.

4. Make the ears and a long, thin tail. Mould them onto your mouse.

5. Finish off by giving it some currant eyes. Now it is ready to eat!

Be careful! Always keep your sugar paste in its wrapper to keep it moist. It will go hard if you leave it out in the air.

21

Baking tips

You may like to do some baking too. If so, ask an adult to help you.

1. Before you begin always wash your hands and put on an apron.

2. To measure liquid use a jug with measurements on the side. Read it at eye level.

3. Use scales to weigh your flour.

4. If you use a knife always cut with the knife facing away from you.

5. When you work with pastry or dough sprinkle the rolling pin and work surface with flour so that the pastry does not stick.

6. Do not open the oven door when things are cooking. Wait until the correct time is up.

Facts about bakers

Richard is a craft baker. This means that in his bakery he both produces and sells bread and cakes on the same day. A craft baker makes, bakes and sells everything in his or her own business. Craft bakeries can be big or small. They produce bread, rolls, sweet and savoury pies and celebration cakes.

Craft bakers have to be able to do many different things and use all kinds of skills each day. They have to be good at working with their hands, able to use complicated equipment and enjoy working in a team.

To become a craft baker you need to have proper training and acquire an NVQ (National Vocational Qualification). Some bakers specialise in one area such as pastries or confectionery.

Index

© 1998 Franklin Watts

Franklin Watts
96 Leonard Street
London
EC2A 4RH

Franklin Watts Australia
14 Mars Road
Lane Cove
NSW 2066

ISBN: 0 7496 2988 6

Dewey Decimal Classification
Number: 664

10 9 8 7 6 5 4 3 2 1

A CIP catalogue record for
this book is available from the
British Library.

Printed in Malaysia

Editor: Samantha Armstrong
Designer: Kirstie Billingham
Photographer: Steve Shott
Illustrations: Richard Morgan

With thanks to: Nicola and
Claire Eastick, Mr Richard
Matthiae and all the staff of
Matthiae's Bakery, Richmond.